the little book of life

E... ... you,
lif... ... which
bit... from.

LIFE

Why am I here?

God is the One who gives life, breath, and everything else to people.

ACTS 17:25

God is the One who gives life, breath, and everything else to people.
ACTS 17:25

You made my whole being; you formed me in my mother's body. You saw my body as it was formed. All the days planned for me were written in your book before I was one day old.

PSALM 139:13, 16

You made my whole being; you formed me in my mother's body. You saw my body as it was formed. All the days planned for me were written in your book before I was one day old.

PSALMS 139:13, 16

Jesus said: "Look at the birds in the sky! They don't plant or harvest. They don't even store grain in barns. Yet your Father in heaven takes care of them. Aren't you worth more than birds?"

MATTHEW 6:26

Jesus said: "Look at the birds in the sky! They don't even store grain in barns. Yet your Father in heaven takes care of them. Aren't you worth more than birds?"

MATTHEW 6:26

SECURITY

Where can I find it?

God cares for you,
so turn all your worries
over to him.

1 PETER 5:7

God cares
for you, so turn
all your worries
over to him.
1 PETER 5:7

SECURITY

Every word of God is true. He guards those who come to him for safety.

PROVERBS 30:5

Every word of God is true. He guards those who come to him for safety.
Proverbs 30:5

Jesus said: "Owning a lot of things won't make your life safe."

LUKE 12:15

Jesus said: "Owning a lot of things won't make your life safe."
LUKE 12:15

Don't worry about anything, but pray about everything. ...God will bless you with peace that no one can completely understand. And this peace will control the way you think and feel.

PHILIPPIANS 4:6-7

Don't worry about anything, but pray about everything. ...God will bless you with peace that no one can completely understand. And this peace will control the way you think and feel.

PHILIPPIANS 4:6-7

LOVE

God says: "Can a woman forget the baby she nurses? Can she feel no kindness for the child to which she gave birth? Even if she could forget her children, I will not forget you."

ISAIAH 49:15

God says: "Can a woman forget the baby she nurses? Can she feel no kindness for the child to which she gave birth? Even if she could forget her children, I will not forget you."
ISAIAH 49:15

LOVE

The LORD loves us very much, and his truth is everlasting.

PSALM 117:2

The LORD loves us very much, and his truth is everlasting.
PSALM 117:2

LOVE

Some friends don't help, but a true friend is closer than your own family.

PROVERBS 18:24

Some friends don't help, but a true friend is closer than your own family.
PROVERBS 18:24

LOVE

The LORD is good. His
love is forever, and his loyalty
goes on and on.

PSALM 100:5

**The LORD
IS** good. His
love is forever,
and his loyalty
goes on and
on.
PSALM 100:5

LOVE

Your (the LORD's)

kindness and love will always
be with me each day of my
life.

PSALM 23:6

Your (the LORD's)
kindness and
love will always
be with me
each day of my
life,
PSALM 23:6

LIFESTYLE

How should I live?

We may think we are doing the right thing, but the LORD always knows what is in our hearts.

PROVERBS 21:2

We may think we are doing the right thing, but the LORD always knows what is in our hearts.
PROVERBS 21:2

With all your heart you must trust the LORD and not your own judgment. Always let him lead you, and he will clear the road for you to follow.

PROVERBS 3:5-6

With all your heart you must trust the LORD and not your own judgment. Always let him lead you, and he will clear the road for you to follow.
PROVERBS 3:5-6

Consider others more important than yourselves. Care about them as much as you care about yourselves.

PHILIPPIANS 2:3-4

Consider others more important than yourselves. Care about them as much as you care about yourselves.

PHILIPPIANS 2:3-4

The LORD God has told us what is right and what he demands: "See that justice is done, let mercy be your first concern, and humbly obey your God."

MICAH 6:8

The LORD God has told us what is right and what he demands: "See that justice is done, let mercy be your first concern, and humbly obey your God."
MICAH 6:8

God says: "Stop doing wrong and learn to live right. See that justice is done."

ISAIAH 1:16-17

God says: "Stop doing wrong and learn to live right. See that justice is done."

ISAIAH 1:16-17

FREEDOM

Where the Spirit of the Lord is, there is freedom.

2 CORINTHIANS 3:17

Where the Spirit of the Lord is, there is freedom.
2 CORINTHIANS 3:17

You must never stop looking at the perfect law that sets you free. God will bless you in everything you do, if you listen and obey, and don't just hear and forget.

JAMES 1:25

You must never stop looking at the perfect law that sets you free. God will bless you in everything you do, if you listen and obey, and don't just hear and forget.
JAMES 1:25

Jesus said: "If you continue to obey my teaching, you are truly my followers.

Then you will know the truth, and the truth will make you free. ...If the Son makes you free, you will be truly free."

JOHN 8:31-32,36

Jesus said: "If you continue to obey my teaching, you are truly my followers. Then you will know the truth, and the truth will make you free. ...If the Son makes you free, you will be truly free."
JOHN 8:31-32,36

Jesus said: "I came to give life – life in all its fullness."

JOHN 10:10

Jesus said: "I came to give life – life in all its fullness."
JOHN 10:10

People who are ruled by their desires think only of themselves. Everyone who is ruled by the Holy Spirit thinks about spiritual things. If our minds are ruled by our desires, we will die. But if our minds are ruled by the Spirit, we will have life and peace.

ROMANS 8:5-6

People who are ruled by their desires think only of themselves. Everyone who is ruled by the Holy Spirit thinks about spiritual things. If our minds are ruled by our desires, we will die. But if our minds are ruled by the Spirit, we will have life and peace.
ROMANS 8:5-6

THOUGHTS

How do I handle them?

Carefully guard your thoughts because they are the source of true life.

PROVERBS 4:23

Carefully guard your thoughts because they are the source of true life.
PROVERBS 4:23

Be changed within by a new way of thinking. Then you will be able to decide what God wants for you; you will know what is good and pleasing to him and what is perfect.

ROMANS 12:2

Be changed within by a new way of thinking. Then you will be able to decide what God wants for you; you will know what is good and pleasing to him and what is perfect.
ROMANS 12:2

THOUGHTS

Think about the things that are true and honourable and right and pure and beautiful and respected. ...And the God who gives peace will be with you.

PHILIPPIANS 4:8-9

Think about the things that are true and honourable and right and pure and beautiful and respected. ...And the God who gives peace will be with you.
PHILIPPIANS 4:8-9

How can a young person live a pure life? By obeying God's word.

PSALM 119:9

How can a young person live a pure life? By obeying God's word.
PSALM 119:9

FAILURE

I know that my selfish desires won't let me do anything that is good. Even when I want to do right, I cannot. Instead of doing what I know is right, I do wrong.

ROMANS 7:18-19

I know that my selfish desires won't let me do anything that is good. Even when I want to do right, I cannot. Instead of doing what I know is right, I do wrong.

ROMANS 7:18-19

FAILURE

If you don't confess your sins, you will be a failure. But God will be merciful if you confess your sins and give them up.

PROVERBS 28:13

If you don't confess your sins, you will be a failure. But God will be merciful if you confess your sins and give them up.
PROVERBS 28:13

FAILURE

If we say that we have not sinned, we are fooling ourselves, and the truth isn't in our hearts. But if we confess our sins to God, he can always be trusted to forgive us and take our sins away.

1 JOHN 1:8-9

If we say that we have not sinned, we are fooling ourselves, and the truth isn't in our hearts. But if we confess our sins to God, he can always be trusted to forgive us and take our sins away.

1 JOHN 1:8-9

God showed his love for us when he sent his only Son into the world to give us life. Real love isn't our love for God, but his love for us. God sent his Son to be the sacrifice by which our sins are forgiven.

1 JOHN 4:9-10

God showed his love for us when he sent his only Son into the world to give us life. Real love isn't our love for God, but his love for us. God sent his Son to be the sacrifice by which our sins are forgiven.
1 JOHN 4:9-10

ACCEPTANCE

God accepts people only because they have faith in Jesus Christ. All of us have sinned and fallen short of God's glory. But God treats us much better than we deserve, and because of Christ Jesus, he freely accepts us and sets us free from our sins.

ROMANS 3:22-24

God accepts people only because they have faith in Jesus Christ. All of us have sinned and fallen short of God's glory. But God treats us much better than we deserve, and because of Christ Jesus, he freely accepts us and sets us free from our sins.
ROMANS 3:22-24

Jesus said: "The Father gives me my people. Every one of them will come to me, and I will always accept them."

JOHN 6:37

Jesus said: "The Father gives me my people. Every one of them will come to me, and I will always accept them."
JOHN 6:37

Money paid to workers isn't a gift. It is something they earn by working. But you cannot make God accept you because of something you do. God accepts sinners only because they have faith in him.

ROMANS 4:4-5

Money paid to workers isn't a gift. It is something they earn by working. But you cannot make God accept you because of something you do. God accepts sinners only because they have faith in him.
ROMANS 4:4-5

Jesus said: "If anyone loves me, they will obey me. Then my Father will love them, and we will come to them and live in them."

JOHN 14:23

Jesus said: "If anyone loves me, they will obey me. Then my Father will love them, and we will come to them and live in them."
JOHN 14:23

RESPONSE

Respect and obey the LORD! This is the beginning of wisdom. To have understanding, you must know the Holy God.

PROVERBS 9:10

Respect and obey the LORD! This is the beginning of wisdom. To have understanding, you must know the Holy God.

PROVERBS 9:10

Turn to God! Give up your sins, and you will be forgiven.

ACTS 3:19

Turn to God! Give up your sins, and you will be forgiven.
ACTS 3:19

Jesus said: "If you try to save your life, you will lose it. But if you give it up for me, you will find it."

MATTHEW 10:39

Jesus said: "If you try to save your life, you will lose it. But if you give it up for me, you will find it."

MATTHEW 10:39

Jesus said: "Ask, and you will receive. Search, and you will find. Knock, and the door will be opened for you. Everyone who asks will receive. Everyone who searches will find. And the door will be opened for everyone who knocks."

MATTHEW 7:7-8

Jesus said: "Ask, and you will receive. Search, and you will find. Knock, and the door will be opened for you. Everyone who asks will receive. Everyone who searches will find. And the door will be opened for everyone who knocks."
MATTHEW 7:7-8

RESPONSE

Jesus said: "Come to me, all of you who are tired and have heavy loads, and I will give you rest. Accept my teachings and learn from me, because I am gentle and humble in spirit, and you will find rest for your lives."

MATTHEW 11:28-29

Jesus said: "Come to me, all of you who are tired and have heavy loads, and I will give you rest. Accept my teachings and learn from me, because I am gentle and humble in spirit, and you will find rest for your lives."

MATTHEW 11:28-29

FUTURE

Can I be sure?

God makes

everything happen at the
right time. Yet none of us can
ever fully understand all he has
done, and he puts questions in our
minds about the past and the future.

ECCLESIASTES 3:11

God makes
everything
happen at the
right time. Yet none
of us can ever fully
understand all he has
done, and he puts
questions in our minds
about the past and the
future.
ECCLESIASTES 3:11

Jesus said: "More than anything else, put God's work first and do what he wants. ...Don't worry about tomorrow. It will take care of itself. You have enough to worry about today."

MATTHEW 6:33-34

Jesus said: "More than anything else, put God's work first and do what he wants....

Don't worry about tomorrow. It will take care of itself. You have enough to worry about today."

MATTHEW 6:33-34

LORD, I trust you.

I have said, "You are my God."
My life is in your hands.

PSALM 31:14-15

LORD, I
trust you.
I have said,
"You are my
God." My life is
in your hands.
PSALM 31:14-15

God has promised us
a new heaven and a new earth,
where justice will rule.

2 PETER 3:13

God has promised us a new heaven and a new earth, where justice will rule.

2 PETER 3:13

FUTURE

I saw a new heaven and
a new earth.... God will wipe
all tears from their eyes, and
there will be no more death, suffering,
crying, or pain. These things of the
past are gone forever.

REVELATION 21:1,4

I saw a new heaven
and a new
earth.... God
will wipe all
tears from their
eyes, and there
will be no more
death, suffering,
crying, or pain.
These things of the
past are gone
forever.
REVELATION 21:1,4

FUTURE

What God has planned for people who love him is more than eyes have seen or ears have heard. It has never even entered our minds!

1 CORINTHIANS 2:9

What God has planned for people who love him is more than eyes have seen or ears have heard. It has never even entered our minds!

1 CORINTHIANS 2:9

What does the Bible say about friends, money, sex, ambition, worry and prayer?

The little book of help is another book in this series. Get in touch if you'd like a free copy.

SGM International
218 York Street   Belfast BT15 1GY
40 Talbot Street   Dublin 1

Printed by BPS.